CANADA

A TRUE BOOK

by
Elaine Landau

Children's Press®

A Division of Grolier Publishing

New York London Hong Kong Sydney
Danbury, Connecticut

Montreal, Quebec

Reading Consultant
Linda Cornwell
Coordinator of School Quality
and Professional Improvement
Indiana State Teachers
Association

Author's Dedication
For Derek Kessler

Visit Children's Press® on the
Internet at:
http://publishing.grolier.com

Library of Congress Cataloging-in-Publication Data

   Canada / by Elaine Landau.
     p.   cm.—(A true book)
   Includes: bibliographical references and index.
   Summary: A basic overview of the history, geography, climate, and
culture of Canada.
   ISBN: 0-516-21170-6 (lib. bdg.)   0-516-27021-4 (pbk.)
   1. Canada—Juvenile literature. [1. Canada] I. Title. II. Series.
F1008.2.L33   1999
971—dc2   99-13662
                                                    CIP
                                                    AC

2385-6759
5/00

GROLIER
PUBLISHING

Contents

A Land Of Contrasts 5

History 10

The People 17

The Economy 26

Government 32

Art and Culture 36

From Sea to Sea 39

To Find Out More 44

Important Words 46

Index 47

Meet the Author 48

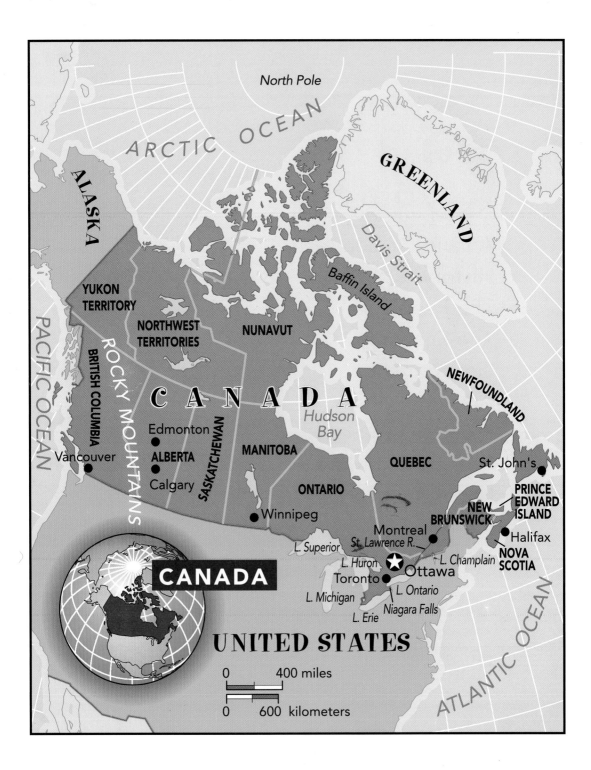

North Pole

ARCTIC OCEAN

GREENLAND

ALASKA

Davis Strait

Baffin Island

YUKON
TERRITORY

NORTHWEST
TERRITORIES

NUNAVUT

PACIFIC OCEAN

BRITISH COLUMBIA

ROCKY MOUNTAINS

C A N A D A

Hudson
Bay

NEWFOUNDLAND

Edmonton

ALBERTA

SASKATCHEWAN

MANITOBA

QUEBEC

St. John's

Calgary

ONTARIO

PRINCE
EDWARD
ISLAND

Vancouver

Winnipeg

Montreal
St. Lawrence R.

NEW
BRUNSWICK

Halifax

L. Superior

NOVA
SCOTIA

L. Champlain

L. Huron

Toronto

Ottawa

L. Michigan

L. Ontario

Niagara Falls

CANADA

L. Erie

UNITED STATES

ATLANTIC OCEAN

0   400 miles

0   600 kilometers

A Land of Contrasts

Picture the continent of North America. Canada, which lies to the north, is the largest country. With an area of 3,849,674 square miles (9,970,610 square kilometers), Canada is the second-largest country in the world. Only Russia is bigger.

Canada has 7 percent of the world's land and 9 percent of its fresh-water supply. Flying over parts of the country you see more water than land. Canada shares four of the Great Lakes with the United States, and there are many other lakes throughout Canada.

Canada is a beautiful country with a varied landscape. There are towering mountains, vast prairies, lush

The Great Lakes

Lake Superior

The Great Lakes consist of six connecting lakes in east-central North America—Lakes Ontario, Erie, Huron, Michigan, Superior, and Champlain. Together, they contain 18 percent of the world's fresh surface water.

Lake Champlain

Baffin Island (top) and Mount Rundle (bottom)

forests, fertile farmland, fishing villages, and bustling cities. The nation is so large that it spans six time zones from coast to coast!

In northern Canada, temperatures are below zero most of the year. But the areas near Canada's southern border tend to have mild springs, hot summers, and pleasantly crisp falls. In many ways, Canada is a land of contrasts.

History

Long before Europeans arrived in Canada, groups of native people lived there. The first inhabitants of Canada probably arrived from Asia more than fifteen thousand years ago. It is believed that they crossed a land bridge that once connected Asia and Alaska. Today, this

Few Inuit families live in igloos today.

bridge is known as the Bering land bridge.

Another group of people may have used the same land bridge to reach Canada's freezing Arctic. These were the ancestors of the Inuit (IN-yoo-it), formerly known as Eskimos. The word Inuit means "the people." The Inuit lived by hunting, fishing, and farming.

In the 1500s, English and French explorers arrived in Canada. The French settlers gave the country the Iroquois name of Canada, or kanata, meaning "the village." They found the waters full of fish. They knew that fur from the abundant beavers, foxes, and bears would be popular in

Europe. By the early 1600s, both England and France had established colonies in what is now Canada. Britain eventually gained control of the region. This brought about 65,000 French-speaking people in Canada under their rule.

On July 1, 1867, four of Britain's Canadian colonies joined together to become the Dominion of Canada. Over time, others followed. While it was still tied to Britain, the Dominion of Canada's government was based on the British system. The new country also began a westward expansion of its territory. In time, it stretched from the Atlantic to the Pacific coast, and included northern territories. Britain granted Canada its full independence in 1931. Newfoundland, the tenth and last province, joined the Dominion in 1949.

Canada's people are as varied as its landscape. Inuit, other North American Indians, and people of French and British descent lived in Canada.

By the end of the 1800s, many immigrants from northern and eastern Europe had also settled there. Large numbers of Chinese and South Asians also arrived in Canada. Many came to work in the mines or on the railroads. Others looked for work in various industries such as fishing and farming. Most arrived hoping to build a better life for themselves and their families.

The People

Despite Canada's large size, about 30 million people live there today. (The United States population is 270 million.) Canada's population is more diverse than ever. According to the 1996 census, only half of the Canadian population has a British or

French ethnic background.
Other groups include
Germans, Italians, Ukrainians,
Dutch, Polish, Chinese, South
Asian, Jewish, Caribbean,

Portuguese, Scandinavian, Inuit, and Canadian Indian.

More than 55,000 Inuit live in fifty-three communities in the Northwest Territories, northern Labrador, and northern Quebec. In recent years this population has grown rapidly. In 1999, half of Canada's vast Northwest Territories became a self-governing Inuit territory called Nunavut (NOO-na-voot), meaning "our land." It is believed that there will be more than 84,000 Inuit living in Canada by 2016.

More than 593,000 other
North American Indians also
live in Canada, making up 608
Indian bands, or "First Nations,"
across the country. Half of
Canada's Indians live on land
areas called reserves that have

been set aside for them. Usually, the reserves are in rural areas and are quite isolated.

Many Canadians live near the country's southern border with the United States. Just as the United States is divided

Chateau Frontenac, Quebec City

Canada's Provinces and Territories

Province	Capital	Population
Alberta	Edmonton	2,696,826
British Columbia	Victoria	3,724,500
Manitoba	Winnipeg	1,113,898
New Brunswick	Fredericton	738,133
Newfoundland	St. John's	551,792
Nova Scotia	Halifax	909,282
Ontario	Toronto	10,753,573
Prince Edward Island	Charlottetown	134,577
Quebec	Quebec City	7,138,795
Saskatchewan	Regina	990,237

Territory	Capital	Population
Northwest Territories	Yellowknife	52,238
Nunavut	Iqaluit	24,000
Yukon Territory	Whitehorse	23,504

into states, Canada is divided into ten provinces and three territories. Each province and territory has its own capital and local government.

Canadian children are required to attend school from age six to sixteen. Some go on to colleges, universities, and technical institutes after high school. A small amount of Canada's working population has a college or university degree. About half of the workforce consists of high-school graduates.

Sports are popular in Canada, especially ice hockey. Some of the world's most

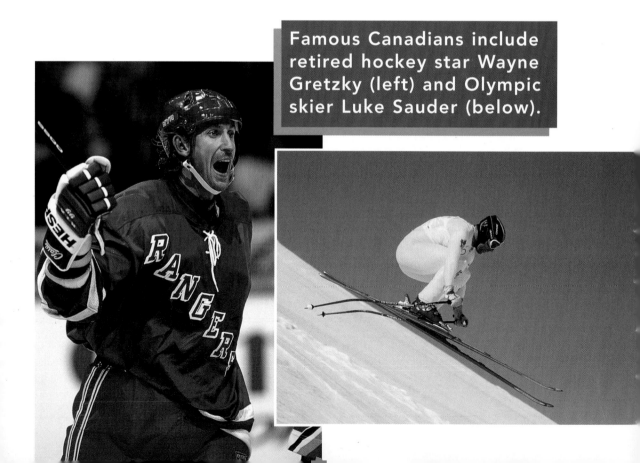

Famous Canadians include retired hockey star Wayne Gretzky (left) and Olympic skier Luke Sauder (below).

famous hockey players come from Canada. Besides playing hockey, many young Canadians enjoy downhill and cross-country skiing, soccer, baseball, tennis, and basketball.

The largest religious group in Canada is Roman Catholic. The second-largest is Protestant. Many other Canadians follow the Jewish, Muslim, Buddhist, Hindu, and Sikh faiths.

The Economy

Trade and international investment are important to Canada's economy. The country is also rich in raw materials, such as copper, gold, silver, platinum, iron, nickel, zinc, coal, petroleum, and natural gas. Canada's main exports include pulp and paper, wood,

An oil refinery in Canada

fuel, minerals, aluminum, wheat, and oil. It is also a major exporter of transportation equipment.

In the country's early days, most Canadians farmed, fished, or trapped animals for their meat and fur. Many people worked as

Fishing and Farming

About 8 percent of Canada's land is used for farming. The main products are wheat, milk, cattle, dairy items, pork, and poultry.

A farm

A wheat field

Fishing crews in the Atlantic and the Pacific oceans bring in large catches of salmon and herring. Perch, pickerel, and whitefish are plentiful in many of Canada's lakes.

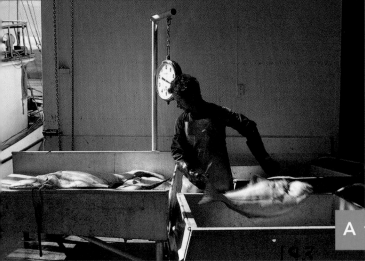

A fish company

loggers. Today, almost half of the country's workers are in the service industry. This includes health care, recreation, education, transportation, communication, government, banking, and other businesses.

Modern advances have changed the lives of the Inuit, too. Most Inuit no longer live in igloos. Today they have houses with central heating, electricity, and plumbing. Snowmobiles and all-terrain trucks have replaced the dog-pulled sleds of the past. And hunting and fishing are no longer so important to the Inuit. An international market for Inuit carvings and prints provides a steady income to many communities. Also, the growth of Inuit communities has provided many jobs in community services, development projects, and government. However, many Inuit and native Indian communities

Houses have replaced igloos for most Inuit families.

are so remote that the residents cannot work in major labor markets. As a result, finding new job opportunities for the growing population remains a challenge.

Government

Did you know that Queen Elizabeth II of England is Canada's queen, too? But Canada is an independent nation, and the queen does not govern it. The governor-general acts as the queen's personal representative and official head of the Canadian Parliament.

Canada's government combines a federal form of government with a parliamentary form of government. The federal government takes care of problems that are common to all of the provinces and territories. Each province or territory also has its own government that handles the special needs of the various areas, such as education, property, and taxation.

Parliament is the country's central government. It takes care

Parliament Hill contains the Senate and the House of Commons.

of such matters as national defense, international trade and commerce, immigration, the banking system, and telecommunications.

Parliament Hill, located in Ottawa, Ontario, (the capital city of Canada), is divided into two sections, the Senate and the House of Commons. The Canadian people elect the members of the House of Commons, who pass laws involving the raising or spending of money and other important matters. Senators are appointed by the governor-general. The Senate can also pass laws, but not on raising or spending money. The leader of the political party that has the largest number of people in the House of Commons becomes the prime minister. The Canadian prime minister runs the government.

Art and Culture

Canada's government actively encourages the arts. For example, it supports the National Arts Center in Ottawa, where music, theater, and dance performances are regularly offered. The government-sponsored Canadian Film Board is known for its award-winning documentaries

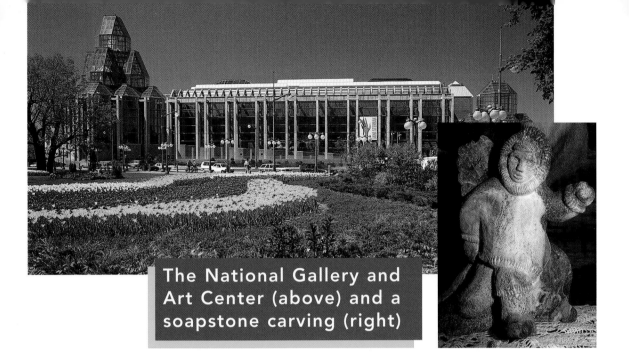

The National Gallery and Art Center (above) and a soapstone carving (right)

and children's films. Canada's National Gallery features the work of many Canadian painters. Numerous Canadian artists such as Tom Thomson, Lucius O'Brien, Emily Carr, and David Milne have captured the beauty and spirit of their country on canvas.

Canada has professional ballet companies and orchestras, as well as many theater and opera companies. In some ways, Canada's art and culture reflect its varied population. Outstanding Canadian literature has been written in both English and French. In addition, markets for Canadian-Indian art and Inuit soapstone carvings have grown enormously in recent years.

From Sea to Sea

People from the United States often feel at home in Canada. The two countries are very much alike in some ways. Many Canadian industries are owned by U.S. companies and citizens. Over the years, however, Canadians have tried not to be overshadowed by their neighbors to the south. They wish to preserve their own unique heritage and culture.

Preserving their culture hasn't always been easy because Canada is made up of so many different groups. The largely French-speaking province of Quebec has passed laws to protect its French language and customs. In fact, many people in Quebec want to make Quebec a separate country. People in other parts of the

Much of the rich French heritage of Quebec has been preserved.

country also want the government to pay more attention to their special needs.

The government has done much to help save the country's heritage. For example, heritage language courses are offered in many communities. And courses on the history and culture of various ethnic groups are now taught in public schools and universities. Radio and television programs geared to special groups have become quite popular as well. In July 1998, the Canadian government passed the Canadian Multicultural Act. This law is designed to ensure that all Canadians are fully represented as the nation goes forward.

Its many and varied groups are part of the fabric of

Canada is a country filled with interesting culture and natural beauty.

Canadian life today. Recognizing their differences as well as their common goals gives everyone a chance to contribute to Canada's unity and well-being.

To Find Out More

Here are some additional resources to help you learn more about the nation of Canada:

 **Books**

Armbruster, Ann. **Lake Superior.** Children's Press, 1996.

Harrison, Ted. **O Canada.** Ticknor & Fields, 1993.

McFarlane, Brian. **Hockey for Kids.** Morrow Books, 1996.

Rootes, David. **The Arctic.** Lerner Publications, 1996.

Tames, Richard. **Journey through Canada.** Troll Associates, 1991.

Wright, David K. **Canada Is My Home.** Gareth Stevens, 1992.

Organizations and Online Sites

Canada From C2C
http://www.canadac2c.com/ kidscybr.html

Dozens of fun links to sites designed for and by Canadian kids. Learn about the country's government, history, weather, libraries, and more.

Cool Sites For Kids Only
http://www.nrcan.gc.ca/edu/

This site features cool games kids can play and provides tons of information about Canada's natural resources.

Discover Canada Online
http://WWW.Discover Canada.COM/

Considered the best website on the Internet about Canada, this site provides information on the best tourist sights in Canada.

Nunavut Fact Facts
http://www.inac.gc.ca/ nunavut/map.html

Get all the facts about Canada's newest territory, Nunavut.

YES Magazine
http://www.yesmag.bc.ca/

Read Canada's science magazine for kids online. Get the latest on "hot" science news, try an experimental project at home, or meet a few Kids In Science. There's also a great resource page for parents and teachers.

Important Words

census an official count of all the people living in a country or district

continent one of Earth's seven great masses of land

ethnic having to do with people of the same race or nationality who share the same language and culture

expansion an increase in size

federal a form of government that is controlled by one central power or authority

igloo the traditional doomed house of the Inuit, often made of hard snow

Parliament a group of people who have been elected to make the laws

remote distant; located in a far-off place

Index

(**Boldface** page numbers
   indicate illustrations.)

Bering land bridge, 11
Canadian Film Board, 36
climate, 9
economy, 26
education, 23, 33
England, 13, 14, 15
Europeans, 10
explorers, 12
exports, 26–27
farming, 12, 16, 28
First Nations, 20, 21
fishing, 12, 16, 28, 30
governor-general, 32, 35
Great Lakes, 6, 7, **7**
House of Commons, 34,
   35
hunting, 12, 30
Inuit, 11, **11,** 12, 15, 19,
   29, 30
Labrador, 19
National Arts Center, 36

National Gallery, 37, **37**
North America, 5, 7
North American Indians,
   15, 20, **20,** 30
Northwest Territories, 19
Nunavut, 19
Ontario, 34
Parliament, 32, 33
Parliament Hill, 34, **34**
population, 17–19
prime minister, 35
provinces, 22, 23, 33
Quebec, 19, 40, **40**
raw materials, 26
religion, 25
reserves, 20
Russia, 5
Senate, 34, 35
soapstone carvings, **37,**
   38
sports, 24–25
territories, 22, 23, 33
United States, 6, 17, 21,
   39

Meet the Author

Popular author Elaine Landau worked as a newspaper reporter, editor, and a youth services librarian before becoming a full-time writer. She has written more than one hundred nonfiction books for young people, including many books for Franklin Watts and Children's Press. Ms. Landau, who has a bachelor's degree in English and journalism from New York University and a master's degree in library and information science from Pratt Institute, lives in Miami, Florida, with her husband and son.